S0-BXJ-875

To _____

Love

From _____

Love

Illustrated by
JUDY PELIKAN

A Welcome Book

Stewart, Tabori & Chang
Publishers, New York

Published in 1994 and distributed in the U.S. by
Stewart, Tabori & Chang, 575 Broadway,
New York, New York 10012

Produced by Welcome Enterprises, Inc.
575 Broadway, New York, New York 10012
Text Research: Sally Seamans, Shannon Rothenberger

1 3 5 7 9 10 8 6 4 2
Printed in Italy

*Grateful acknowledgment is made to the following for permission to
reprint previously published material:*

Open Secret by Maulana Jalalu'ddin Rumi, translated by John
Mayne, Threshold Books, RD 4, Box 600, Putney, VT 05346

The Ruins of the Heart by Maulana Jalalu'ddin Rumi, translated
by Edmund Heminiski, Threshold Books, RD 4, Box 600,
Putney, VT 05346

Poem by Ishikawa Takuboku, reprinted from *Japanese Love
Poems* edited by Jean Bennett. Copyright © 1976 by Doubleday
and Company, Inc.

Letters to a Young Poet excerpt. Reprinted from *Letters To A
Young Poet* by Rainer Maria Rilke, translated by M. D. Herter
Norton, by permission of W. W. Norton & Company, Inc.
Copyright © 1934 by W. W. Norton & Company, Inc.
Copyright renewed 1962 by M. D. Herter Norton. Revised
Edition copyright © 1954 by W. W. Norton & Company, Inc.
Copyright renewed 1982 by M. D. Herter Norton.

LOVE

is the river of life in this world. Think not that ye know it who stand at the little tinkling rill, the first small fountain.

talking to yourself a talk worth keeping
and you put it away for a keen keeping
and you find it to be a hoarding
and you give it away and yet it stays hoarded

like a book read over and over again
like one book being a long row of books
like leaves of windflowers bending low
and bending to be never broken

CARL SANDBURG
Love is a Deep and a Dark and a Lonely

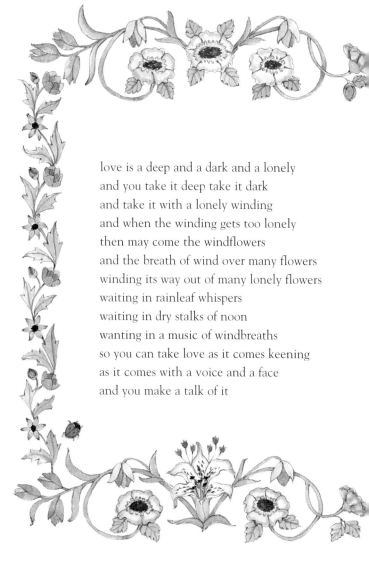

love is a deep and a dark and a lonely
and you take it deep take it dark
and take it with a lonely winding
and when the winding gets too lonely
then may come the windflowers
and the breath of wind over many flowers
winding its way out of many lonely flowers
waiting in rainleaf whispers
waiting in dry stalks of noon
wanting in a music of windbreaths
so you can take love as it comes keening
as it comes with a voice and a face
and you make a talk of it

IT

is good to love many things, for therein
lies the true strength, and whosoever
loves much performs much, and can
accomplish much, and what is done in
love is well done!

VINCENT VAN GOGH
Letter to his brother Theo, May 1877

EEK

Love in the pity of others' woe,
In the gentle relief of another's care,
In the darkness of night and the
    winter's snow,
In the naked and outcast, seek Love there.

WILLIAM BLAKE
Where to Seek Love

anguish(imagine
Her least never with most
memory)give entirely each
Forever its freedom

(Dare until a flower,
understanding sizelessly sunlight
Open what thousandth why and
discover laughing)

E. E. CUMMINGS

be of love(a little)
More careful
Than of everything
guard her perhaps only

A trifle less
(merely beyond how very)
closely than
Nothing,remember love by frequent

FINALLY he walked all the way to the capital to speak to the royal gardener at the sheik's palace. The wise old man had counseled many gardeners before and suggested a variety of remedies to expel the dandelions but Mulla had tried them all. They sat together in silence for some time and finally the gardener looked at Nasrudin and said, "Well, then I suggest you learn to love them."

SUFI TRADITION

ULLA

Nasrudin decided to start a flower garden.
He prepared the soil and planted the
seeds of many beautiful flowers. But
when they came up, his garden was
filled not just with his chosen flowers
but also overrun by dandelions. He
sought out advice from gardeners all
over and tried every method known to
get rid of them but to no avail.

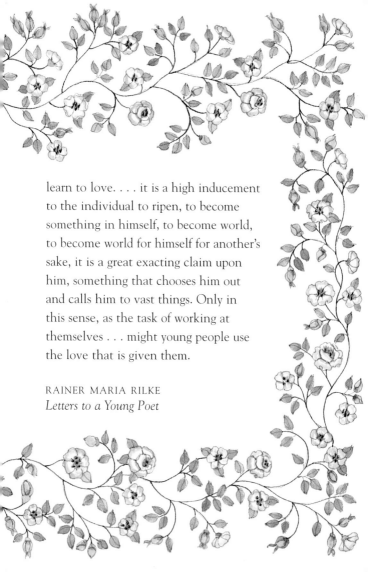

learn to love. . . . it is a high inducement
to the individual to ripen, to become
something in himself, to become world,
to become world for himself for another's
sake, it is a great exacting claim upon
him, something that chooses him out
and calls him to vast things. Only in
this sense, as the task of working at
themselves . . . might young people use
the love that is given them.

RAINER MARIA RILKE
Letters to a Young Poet

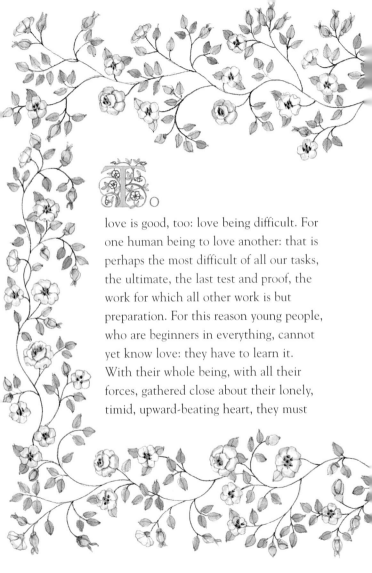

To
love is good, too: love being difficult. For
one human being to love another: that is
perhaps the most difficult of all our tasks,
the ultimate, the last test and proof, the
work for which all other work is but
preparation. For this reason young people,
who are beginners in everything, cannot
yet know love: they have to learn it.
With their whole being, with all their
forces, gathered close about their lonely,
timid, upward-beating heart, they must

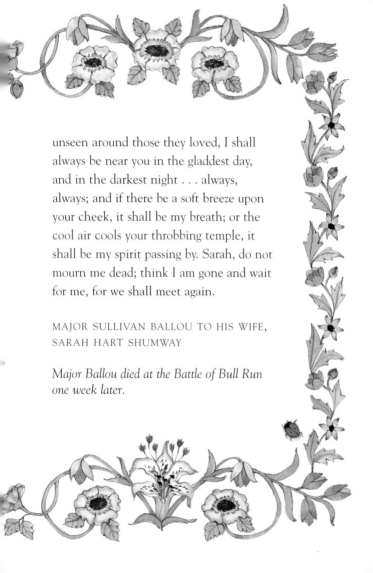

unseen around those they loved, I shall always be near you in the gladdest day, and in the darkest night . . . always, always; and if there be a soft breeze upon your cheek, it shall be my breath; or the cool air cools your throbbing temple, it shall be my spirit passing by. Sarah, do not mourn me dead; think I am gone and wait for me, for we shall meet again.

MAJOR SULLIVAN BALLOU TO HIS WIFE, SARAH HART SHUMWAY

Major Ballou died at the Battle of Bull Run one week later.

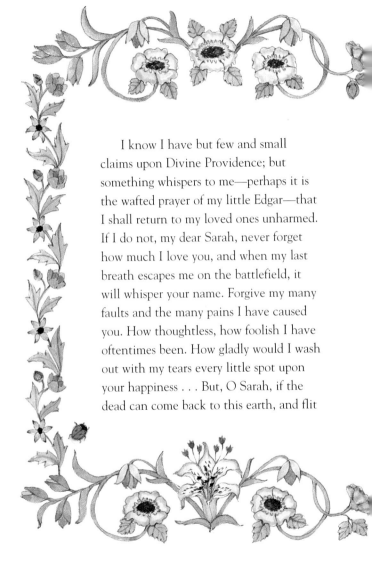

I know I have but few and small
claims upon Divine Providence; but
something whispers to me—perhaps it is
the wafted prayer of my little Edgar—that
I shall return to my loved ones unharmed.
If I do not, my dear Sarah, never forget
how much I love you, and when my last
breath escapes me on the battlefield, it
will whisper your name. Forgive my many
faults and the many pains I have caused
you. How thoughtless, how foolish I have
oftentimes been. How gladly would I wash
out with my tears every little spot upon
your happiness . . . But, O Sarah, if the
dead can come back to this earth, and flit

Washington, Camp Clarke
July 14th, 1861

My very dear Sarah,

HE
indications are very strong that we shall
move in a few days—perhaps tomorrow.
Lest I should not be able to write to you
again, I feel impelled to write a few lines
that may fall under your eye when I shall
be no more. . . .

HERE
are no little events with the heart.
It magnifies everything; it places in
the same scales the fall of an empire
of fourteen years and the dropping
of a woman's glove, and almost always
the glove weighs more than the empire.

HONORE DE BALZAC

wish to feel a love
Which might be likened to
Burying a hot cheek
In a soft drift of snow

ISHIKAWA TAKUBOKU

This is love: to fly toward a secret sky,
to cause a hundred veils to fall each moment.

IRST
to let go of life.
Finally, to take a step without feet.

MAULANA JALALU'DDIN RUMI
The Ruins of The Heart

The minute I heard my first love story
I started looking for you, not knowing
how blind that was.

LOVERS

don't finally meet somewhere.
They're in each other all along.

MAULANA JALALU'DDIN RUMI
Open Secret

WHAT

greater thing is there for two human
souls than to feel that they are joined . . .
to strengthen each other . . . to be at
one with each other in silent unspeakable
memories.

GEORGE ELIOT

THE
truth [is] that there is only one terminal
dignity—love. And the story of a love is
not important—what is important is that
one is capable of love. It is perhaps the
only glimpse we are permitted of eternity.

HELEN HAYES

NOT until you have gone through the rocky gorges, and not lost the stream; not until you have gone through the meadow, and the stream has widened and deepened until fleets could ride on its bosom; not until beyond the meadow you have come to the unfathomable ocean, and poured your treasures into its depths—not until then can you know what love is.

HENRY WARD BEECHER

 ILD

Nights—Wild Nights!
Were I with thee
Wild Nights should be
Our luxury!

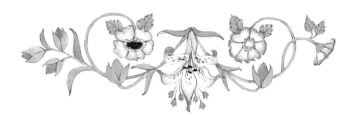

FUTILE—the Winds—
To a Heart in port—
Done with the Compass—
Done with the Chart!

ROWING in Eden—
Ah, the Sea!
Might I but moor—Tonight—
In Thee!

EMILY DICKINSON

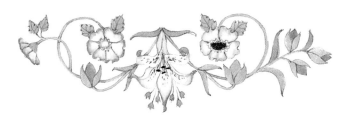

F

I speak in the tongues of men and angels, but have not love, I am a noisy gong or a clanging cymbal. And if I have prophetic powers and understand all mysteries and possess all knowledge, and if I have faith, so as to remove mountains, but have not love, I am nothing.

If I give away all I have, and if I deliver my body to be burned, but have not love, I am nothing.

ST. PAUL
First Epistle to the Corinthians

SOMEWHERE
there waiteth in this world of ours
For one lone soul another lonely soul,
Each choosing each through all the
    weary hours,
And meeting strangely at one sudden goal,

THEN blend they, like green
    leaves with golden flowers,
Into one beautiful and perfect whole;

AND life's long night is ended,
    and the way
Lies open onward to eternal day.

EDWIN ARNOLD
Somewhere There Waiteth

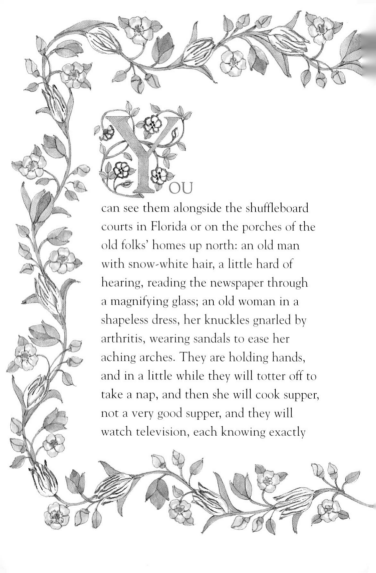

YOU can see them alongside the shuffleboard courts in Florida or on the porches of the old folks' homes up north: an old man with snow-white hair, a little hard of hearing, reading the newspaper through a magnifying glass; an old woman in a shapeless dress, her knuckles gnarled by arthritis, wearing sandals to ease her aching arches. They are holding hands, and in a little while they will totter off to take a nap, and then she will cook supper, not a very good supper, and they will watch television, each knowing exactly

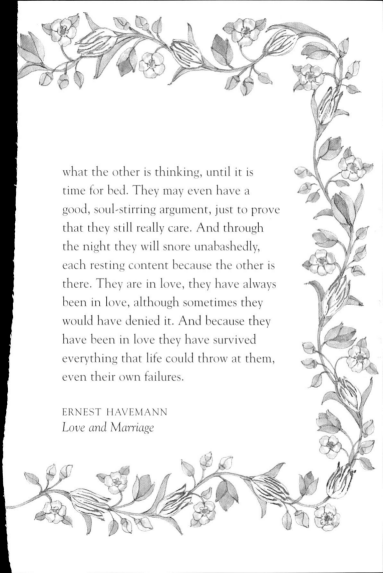

what the other is thinking, until it is
time for bed. They may even have a
good, soul-stirring argument, just to prove
that they still really care. And through
the night they will snore unabashedly,
each resting content because the other is
there. They are in love, they have always
been in love, although sometimes they
would have denied it. And because they
have been in love they have survived
everything that life could throw at them,
even their own failures.

ERNEST HAVEMANN
Love and Marriage

EVERYBODY

can be great . . . because anybody can serve. You don't have to have a college degree to serve. You don't have to make your subject and verb agree to serve. You only need a heart full of grace. A soul generated by love.

MARTIN LUTHER KING, JR.
Strength to Love

A coward is incapable of exhibiting love;
it is the prerogative of the brave.

MOHANDAS (MAHATMA) GANDHI

YOU

will remember that leaping stream
where sweet aromas rose and trembled,
and sometimes a bird, wearing water
and slowness, its winter feathers.

You will remember those gifts from
     the earth:
indelible scents, gold clay,
weeds in the thicket and crazy roots,
magical thorns like swords.

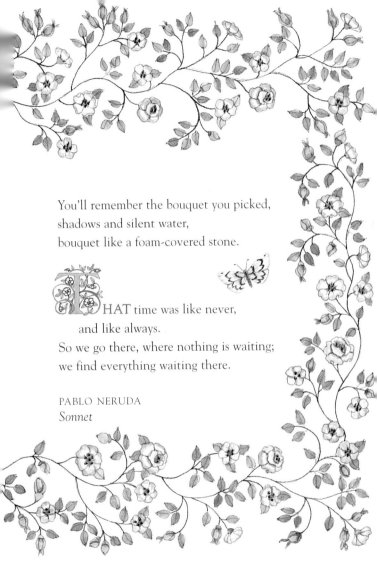

You'll remember the bouquet you picked,
shadows and silent water,
bouquet like a foam-covered stone.

THAT time was like never,
and like always.
So we go there, where nothing is waiting;
we find everything waiting there.

PABLO NERUDA
Sonnet

WHETHER

in Paris, Texas, or Paris, France, we all want to have good jobs where we are needed and respected and paid just a little more than we deserve. We want healthy children, safe streets, to be loved, and have the unmitigated gall to accept love . . .

. . . and someplace to party on Saturday nights.

MAYA ANGELOU
Statement to an Ohio college audience, December, 1993

 heart is not judged by how much you love, but by how much you are loved by others.

NOEL LANGLEY, FLORENCE RYERSON,
EDGAR ALLAN WOLFE
The Wizard of Oz (Motion Picture)

WHAT

is REAL?" asked the Rabbit one day when they were lying side by side near the nursery fender, before Nana came to tidy the room. "Does it mean having things that buzz inside you and a stick-out handle?"

"Real isn't how you are made," said the Skin Horse. "It's a thing that happens to you. When a child loves you for a long, long time, not just to play with, but REALLY loves you, then you become Real."

"Does it hurt?" asked the Rabbit.

"Sometimes," said the Skin Horse, for he was always truthful. "When you are Real you don't mind being hurt."

DOES it happen all at once, like being wound up," he asked, "or bit by bit?"

"It doesn't happen all at once," said the Skin Horse. "You become. It takes a long time. That's why it doesn't often happen to people who break easily, or have sharp edges, or who have to be carefully kept.

GENERALLY, by the time you are Real, most of your hair has been loved off, and your eyes drop out and you get loose in the joints and very shabby. But these things don't matter at all, because once you are Real, you can't be ugly, except to people who don't understand."

MARGERY WILLIAMS
The Velveteen Rabbit

OTHING
is impossible to a willing heart.

JOHN HEYWOOD